ADOPTING A DOG Quarterly

By Jan Mahood

Have you been wanting a dog but were unsure of what kind of dog you wanted? Adopting a Dog Quarterly gives you insight to a world of dogs that are missing out on the opportunity of enlightening someone's life. With a visit to your local shelter or rescue it could be you or your family's lives that become enriched. This Quarterly informs you of the many ways available of finding a new canine best friend. It covers everything from how to choose the type of dog that best fits your lifestyle, to visiting a shelter, contacting rescue agencies and searching the world wide web. Adopting a Dog Quarterly will help start you on the road to dog ownership, as well as teach you how to care for and train your newly adopted companion.

What are Quarterlies?

Books, the usual way information of this sort is transmitted, can be too slow. Sometimes by the book is written and published, the material contained therein is a year or two old...and no new material has been added during that time. Only a book in a magazine form can bring breaking stories and current information. A magazine is streamlined in production, so we have adopted certain magazine publishing techniques in the creation of this yearBOOK. Magazines also can be much cheaper than books because they are supported by advertising. To combine these asstes into a great publication, we issued this yearBOOK in both magazine and book format at different prices.

Distributed in the UNITED STATES to the Pet Trade by T.F.H. Publications, Inc., One T.F.H. Plaza, Neptune City, NJ 07753; distributed in the UNITED STATES to the Bookstore and Library Trade by National Book Network, Inc. 4720 Boston Way, Lanham MD 20706; in CANADA to the Pet Trade by H & L Pet Supplies Inc., 27 Kingston Crescent, Kitchener, Ontario N2B 2T6; Rolf C. Hagen Inc., 3225 Sartelon St. Laurent-Montreal Quebec H4R 1E8; in CANADA to the Book Trade by Vanwell Publishing Ltd., 1 Northrup Crescent, St. Catharines, Ontario L2M 6P5 ; in ENGLAND by T.F.H. Publications, PO Box 15, Waterlooville PO7 6BQ; in AUSTRALIA AND THE SOUTH PACIFIC by T.F.H. (Australia), Pty. Ltd., Box 149, Brookvale 2100 N.S.W., Australia; in NEW ZEALAND by Brooklands Aquarium Ltd. 5 McGiven Drive, New Plymouth, RD1 New Zealand; in Japan by T.F.H. Publications, Japan—Jiro Tsuda, 10-12-3 Ohjidai, Sakura, Chiba 285, Japan; in SOUTH AFRICA by Lopis (Pty) Ltd., P.O. Box 39127, Booysens, 2016, Johannesburg, South Africa. Published by T.F.H. Publications, Inc.
MANUFACTURED IN THE
UNITED STATES OF AMERICA
BY T.F.H. PUBLICATIONS, INC.

yearBOOKS, INC.
Dr. Herbert R. Axelrod,
Founder & Chairman

Neal Pronek
Chief Editor

Kevin Manning
Editor

yearBOOKS are all photo composed, color separated and designed on Scitex equipment in Neptune, N.J. with the following staff:

DIGITAL PRE-PRESS
Patricia Northrup
Supervisor

Robert Onyrscuk
Jose Reyes

COMPUTER ART
Patti Escabi
Sandra Taylor Gale
Candida Moreira
Joanne Muzyka
Francine Shulman

ADVERTISING SALES
George Campbell
National Advertising Manager
Amy Manning
Advertising Director
Sandy Cutillo
Advertising Coordinator
Nancy Rivadeneira
*Periodicals Advertising
Sales Manager*
Cheryl Blyth
*Periodicals Sales
Representative*

©yearBOOKS, Inc.
1 TFH Plaza
Neptune, N.J. 07753
Completely manufactured in
Neptune, N.J. USA

Cover design by Sherise Buhagiar

Whether you adopt your new dog as a puppy or an adult, he will look to you for affection and leadership.

CONTENTS

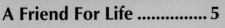

A Friend For Life 5

How to Make the Right Choice 8

Where Are All the Dogs? 16

Dogs.Com: Rescue on
the Internet 28

Bringing Baby Home ... 32

The Healthy Dog 45
Suggested Reading 64

Basic Training for Your Dog 52

Before you bring your new friend home, make sure that you and your family are ready for the responsibility.

A FRIEND FOR LIFE

Before you ask, "What dog is right for me?" take time to explore the question, "Am I ready for a dog?" A careful survey of your needs and resources will help you adopt a healthy dog or puppy that will spend a long, happy life with you.

If you've ever had a dog, you're already well acquainted with the joys and responsibilities that go into dog ownership. If this will be your first dog, brace yourself for:

Joy: Snuggling a new puppy.

Responsibility: House-training a puppy; cleaning up messes.

Joy: Admiring your dog's gleaming coat, athletic body and clear eyes.

Responsibility: Making sure your dog gets proper nutrition, grooming and veterinary care.

Joy: Having your dog run to you when you call him.

Responsibility: Hours, days and weeks of training.

Joy: Taking your dog with you wherever you go —even to hotels that allow dogs!

Responsibility: Earning your dog's trust. Teaching your dog to be a good canine citizen.

BEFORE YOU VISIT THE SHELTER

Every joyful experience results from a serious commitment of precious resources—time and money —on your part. Are you and every member of your family willing to share the responsibility as well as the joy? Get everyone in your household together. With this checklist in hand, ask these questions:

Do we really want a dog? Now's the time to be completely honest with yourself. Do you really love dogs, or are you in love with the idea of having a dog around the house?

Can you afford a dog? Expenses might include an adoption fee, neutering or spaying, registration, veterinary care, food, medications, grooming supplies, toys, training fees, equipment and

Companionship is one of the rewards of dog ownership.

Nurturing your dog is an important part of dog ownership.

transportation. The average yearly amount a family spends on one dog is about $150, but a tab of more than $1,000 a year for a family dog is not unusual. You'll spend the most right after you adopt your dog and during the last year of his life.

If you travel often, you'll have the additional expense of a dog sitter or a boarding kennel. If your dog will spend more than a few hours a day alone, you'll want to think about a fee for a professional dog sitter or gifts for a knowledgeable neighbor who will come once or twice a day to exercise and play with him.

Will a family member be at home at all times? If not, what provisions can be made for your dog's safety, comfort and companionship?

Do you have a secure well-fenced yard? If not, can you afford to install fencing?

If you live in an apartment or close to your neighbors, what noise level is acceptable?

Are dogs permitted in your apartment building or rented house?

Are you willing to get up in the middle of the night or at the crack of dawn to take the dog outside or to care for him when he is ill?

Do you have children? Are any family members elderly? Does anyone in the household have a disability or special need? There may be certain breeds or kinds of dogs that are more appropriate than others for these situations.

Are you willing to teach children to care for the dog, rather than to do everything yourself because it's easier?

Will everyone agree to be consistent regarding the dog's training and behavior? When you say, "The sofa is off-limits!" or "No begging at the table!" will other family members be consistent and back you up?

Will you make sure your

dog gets regular exercise?

Can you afford the time to train your dog and the expense of basic obedience lessons?

Will you clip nails, brush teeth, bathe and groom your dog? Will that long, thick coat that looked so beautiful at the shelter become matted and dull because no one has the time to care for it?

What canine temperament fits your personality? What size and activity level match your physical characteristics? Can you handle a large dog? Do you enjoy jogging, strenuous outdoor play, taking long walks?

What age is best for your family? An exuberant puppy who loves to chew everything in sight and needs to be trained from scratch? A mature dog who may be settled and steady but will probably have to be trained out of some bad habits? An elderly dog who needs love and comfort in his declining years?

Will you take the time to learn about various breeds, or do you prefer an "all-American" mutt? If you've decided on a certain breed,

Caring for your dog is a full-time job. Do you and your family have the time to meet the commitment?

Many questions need to be answered before you bring your new dog home. Do you have the room and the physical strength to care for a large mixed breed?

are you thoroughly familiar with that breed? Have you researched its characteristics? Have you talked with several responsible owners or knowledgeable breeders?

Do you prefer a male or female?

Does anyone in your household suffer from allergies?

Do all agree that they'll eagerly accept not only the joy of having a best friend but also the responsibility of being a best friend?

A COMMITMENT FOR LIFE—YOURS AND THE DOG'S

Owning a dog is a serious commitment. Some of the giant-sized dogs live seven or eight years, some medium-sized dogs live to be 14 or 15, and some small breeds live as long as 18 years or more. That's a long-term relationship! No matter what happens to you—relocation, divorce, illness, injury—you are responsible for the welfare of your dog, a creature who trusts you and depends on you totally for his health and well-being. And if the dog should outlive you, provision should be made for transfer of ownership to someone who will love and care for the dog as you have. Will you make your wishes known in your will?

A MAJOR LIFESTYLE CHANGE

If you've never had a dog before, you are about to undergo a major life change. Are you ready?

No more sleeping until 10 a.m. No more taking off on the spur of the moment for a long skiing weekend. No more relaxing with a good book or favorite T.V. program when it's time for training or a walk. No more immaculate house. Pangs of guilt if you don't spend enough time with your dog. Probably a sharp decline in friends who aren't "dog people!"

More love. More companionship. More fun. More sunrises. More fresh air, exercise and fitness. More new experiences. More new friends.

Opening your door and your heart to a dog will require you to develop your self-discipline, patience, even-handedness and sense of humor. Could it be that a dog, in the process of becoming your best friend, can also help you become a better person?

Make sure you have the activity level to match that of your new dog.

HOW TO MAKE THE RIGHT CHOICE

You've seen people who look like their dogs. This is not always accidental. Although there are no scientific studies to prove this phenomenon exists, it's apparent that dogs and people who live closely over time pick up each other's attitudes and, to a certain extent, appearances.

People often choose dogs whose personality fits theirs, or whose facial expression, coat color or style may even resemble their own. Dogs who sleep most of the day may broaden to look like their sedentary human friends. Joggers' dogs are lean and well-muscled from running beside their fitness-conscious masters. Perhaps the woman with the bulging eyes chose the Boston Terrier because she thought it perfectly beautiful. The swaggering, barrel-chested individual may have picked a massive breed for its intimidating looks.

In selecting canine as well as human companions, beauty often is in the eye of the beholder. The pup out there waiting for you to claim him has a personality—and maybe even an appearance— something like yours. It makes sense to look for a dog who will enjoy the same surroundings and activities that you do. This will be your first step in forming a close bond with your dog.

Every breed was originally developed for a purpose and possesses certain characteristics. The Rottweiler was developed in Germany hundreds of years ago to pull heavily-loaded carts for his master, and has an inbred desire to work. The English Springer Spaniel was bred to flush game birds from brush. He loves to cover an open field from side to side when his human companion takes him out for a run. The aristocratic Italian Greyhound was bred to

There's no limit to the relationship you can share with man's best friend. Arthur was best man at Rick and Mei Ling's wedding.

be an elegant and affectionate companion. After you've chosen a breed you like, you might also see an adoptable all-American mix that closely resembles that breed, but whose size, temperament, coat or cost is better for you and your family.

To learn about the individual characteristics of each breed, look in a library or store for a book such as *Choosing a Dog for Life* or *The Atlas of Dog Breeds.* There are other information-packed books as well that describe all the breeds recognized by the American Kennel Club (AKC), Canadian Kennel Club, United Kennel Club (UKC), the Kennel Club of Great Britain and other registries.

The AKC is the largest registry of purebred dogs in this country. The Fédéracion Cynologique Internacionale (FCI) recognizes the most breeds worldwide. Some purebred dogs that are popular in their own countries are relatively unknown here, and might go unrecognized and be listed as mixed breeds in pounds or shelters.

Friends and acquaintenances who have dogs are a good source of information. Don't hesitate to ask them about the negatives as well as the positives.

Other sources of information are dog magazines and breed videotapes. Breed clubs are another source of information. Each breed has a national breed club and regional clubs made up of breeders, owners and other individuals who have an interest in a particular breed. Examples are the Field Spaniel Society of America, the German Shepherd Club of America and the Miniature Pinscher Club of America. Call or write several breed clubs for literature on breeds that interest you. You can obtain a list of clubs by contacting the AKC.

Your mixed breed can be just as accomplished in the agility ring as his pure-bred cousins.

There are also all-breed dog clubs such as the Westbury (N.Y.) Kennel Association, the Silver Bay Kennel Club of San Diego and the Tennessee Valley Kennel Club. There is probably an all-breed club near you that gives at least one show a year. Find out when the shows are. They provide a great opportunity for you to see every breed of dog and talk to knowledgeable breeders and owners. In addition to watching the dogs in the conformation rings, you can see which breeds usually are good at Obedience. Many shows also feature Agility demonstrations. In this sport, purebred dogs and their mixed-breed cousins, along with their owners, negotiate—usually at full speed—a course of hurdles and other obstacles.

If you're in New York City for National Dog Week in April, stop by Madison Square Park, where the AKC holds its annual Dog Day Afternoon. AKC employees answer questions about various breeds and dogs show off their good looks and skills.

When you've decided which breed or breeds you like best, you can gain additional knowledge from books on the individual breeds or from the national club representing the breed.

If you choose an all-American mutt as your friend for life, you'll see that he probably resembles one of the breeds you've learned about. If you already know something about that breed, you'll understand some aspects of your dog's behavior.

GOOD SPORTS

Setters, spaniels, pointers and retrievers are classified as Sporting dogs and are bred to work with their human companions, hunting and retrieving game birds in field, brush and water. They need daily exercise, enjoy the outdoors, are eager to please and, therefore, are relatively easy to train. They are happiest when involved in outdoor activities with their human companions. Most Sporting dogs quickly adapt to family life, and easily get along with people of all ages. The longer-coated breeds require grooming. Be prepared to gently pull burrs from their coats after a day outside.

Twenty-four Sporting breeds are recognized by the AKC. They are: Brittany, Pointer, German Shorthaired Pointer, German Wirehaired Pointer, Chesapeake Bay Retriever, Curly-Coated Retriever, Flat-Coated Retriever, Golden Retriever, Labrador Retriever, English Setter, Gordon Setter, Irish Setter, American Water Spaniel, Clumber Spaniel, Cocker Spaniel, English Cocker Spaniel, English Springer Spaniel, Field Spaniel, Irish Water Spaniel, Sussex Spaniel, Welsh Springer Spaniel, Vizsla, Weimaraner and Wirehaired Pointing Griffon.

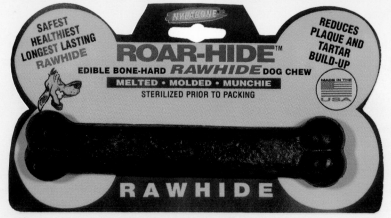

THE NOSE KNOWS

Hounds love the outdoors and are happiest sniffing and tracking, their sensitive noses to the ground, or chasing game at a full gallop, their eyes on their prey. After a day's activity in the fresh air, they enjoy a nap by the fire. They love being with their people, and are unhappy if left alone in the house. Good family dogs, they can be particularly fond of children.

There are two kinds of hounds: Sighthounds, which use their eyes to track game, and Scenthounds, which use their noses. AKC Sighthound breeds are Afghan Hound, Basenji, Borzoi, Greyhound, Ibizan Hound, Irish Wolfhound, Norwegian Elkhound, Pharaoh Hound, Rhodesian Ridgeback, Saluki, Scottish Deerhound and Whippet.

Because of their great speed, Greyhounds and Whippets are used for track racing. When their brief careers are over, they have nowhere to go unless someone adopts them. There are always more Greyhounds and Whippets than there are homes for them. Several organizations around the country rescue retired racing hounds and place them in new homes. Although these dogs love to run, even large Greyhounds are content in surprisingly small quarters because they are used to living in crates at the track. They have gentle, loving natures. People who have rescued Greyhounds and Whippets say that the dogs spend the rest of their lives saying "thank you" to their owners for saving their lives and giving them good homes.

Daily exercise and plenty of outdoor activity is all it takes to keep your sporting dog happy.

If you're attracted to the elegant beauty of the Sighthounds, remember that they are fast! Keep them on a leash when you're outdoors, and try to find a large fenced area near your home where dogs are allowed to run free.

Hounds that follow their noses are also popular household companions. AKC-recognized Scenthound breeds are: Basset Hound, Beagle, Black and Tan Coonhound, Bloodhound, Dachshund, American Foxhound, English Foxhound, Harrier, Otterhound and Petit Basset Griffon Vendéen. These loyal, good-natured dogs love their families. If they catch a tempting scent, however, they're gone! Be sure your property is securely fenced, and instruct children and visitors never to leave an outside door open. Be prepared to give your hound plenty of daily exercise. Also, keep in mind that grooming

Understanding the background of your mixed breed will give you insight to the dog's behavior.

Working breeds require a firm hand, and lots of room and exercise to be happy. Make sure your living situation is appropriate for the dog of your choice.

the coated breeds will be a major investment in time.

SITUATION WANTED

The Working breeds like to have a job to do, whether it's guarding your family, fetching the paper or pulling a cart. These dogs are not for the inexperienced owner, because they need early training and a firm hand. To gain their respect, you need to let them know you are the leader. These dogs are happy with lots of exercise and plenty of room. The largest Working dogs are unsuitable for any but the most spacious homes and grounds. If you live in an apartment, consider another choice. Sad to say, the giant breeds have a reltively short lifespan.

You may want a Working dog or Herding dog if you are looking for a guard dog for your home and family. Akitas, Dobermans and Rottweilers are most commonly used from the Working group for that purpose. However, these breeds are most often relinquished and destroyed because owners couldn't deal with the natural aggressiveness that was emphasized by improper training. These are not dogs for first-time owners.

The 20 Working dogs recognized by the AKC are: Akita, Alaskan Malamute, Bernese Mountain Dog, Boxer, Bullmastiff, Doberman Pinscher, Giant Schnauzer, Great Dane, Great Pyrenees, Greater Swiss Mountain Dog, Komondor, Kuvasz, Mastiff, Newfoundland, Portuguese Water Dog, Rottweiler, Saint Bernard, Samoyed, Siberian Husky and Standard Schnauzer.

HOT DIGGEDY DOGS

Terriers are full of fun and always busy chasing, romping and digging. Their name derives from *terra*—the Latin word for ground, and they were originally bred to go to ground—or into a hole—after small wild animals they hunted with their human companions. They can be fiercely loyal, but also determined, so you'll need to avoid a battle of the wills by instituting a gentle but firm training program. Some terrier breeds are better than others for a home with children. And the terriers commonly used as guard dogs —the Staffordshire Bull Terrier and American Staffordshire Terrier—are not for the inexperienced trainer.

A healthy terrier will live to be 15 years old or older. Terriers come in all shapes and sizes, from the large Airedale down to the Norfolk and Norwich, both close to the ground. Terriers tend to be scrappy, and even the smallest breed may take on a much larger dog, so you'll need to avoid such situations. To keep your terrier's coat looking spiffy, you'll want to learn some specialized grooming techniques that you will use often. You must have either the time to do this or the money for a professional groomer.

There are 25 AKC-recognized terrier breeds from which to choose: Airedale Terrier, American Staffordshire Terrier, Australian Terrier, Bedlington Terrier, Border Terrier, Bull Terrier, Cairn Terrier, Dandie Dinmont Terrier, Smooth Fox Terrier, Wire Fox Terrier, Irish Terrier, Kerry Blue Terrier, Lakeland Terrier, Manchester Terrier, Miniature Bull Terrier, Miniature Schnauzer, Norfolk Terrier, Norwich Terrier, Scottish Terrier, Sealyham Terrier, Skye Terrier, Soft Coated Wheaten Terrier, Staffordshire Bull Terrier, Welsh Terrier and West Highland White Terrier.

A breed recognized by the FCI and KC is the Parson Jack Russell Terrier, a high-spirited bundle of energy. He may be available for adoption because his owner had trouble keeping up with him. The Toy Fox Terrier and Rat Terrier are also lively small dogs that are good watch dogs and lovable pets. If you give these intelligent dogs the training and attention they deserve, they'll reward you by becoming your lifelong pals. And what fun you'll have!

GOOD THINGS IN SMALL PACKAGES

Most Toy breeds were developed as companions and watch dogs. They are fond of home and hearth, and are affectionate little snugglers.

They are intelligent, but can be a challenge to train. This could be because owners tend to "baby" them because they are so small and cute, and do not ask as much of them as they would a larger, stronger dog. Or it simply may be that these breeds act independently to make up for their small size. Most love

Dogs are pack animals and need a leader to understand their place. Who wouldn't want to lead this little guy home?

children, but you must teach youngsters to be gentle with them, because they are small and easily injured. Also, if a small dog is cornered in play by a child, he might nip in self-defense.

Although Toy breeds like a brisk walk as much as anyone, most require little exercise and are well adapted to apartment life. In city, suburb or country, they should always be kept in a fenced area or on lead, because these spirited little dogs are likely to challenge

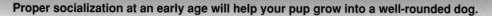

Proper socialization at an early age will help your pup grow into a well-rounded dog.

Honey, a five-year-old rescue female, is jumping for joy at the chance of finding a new home.

much larger dogs or to defend their masters without a thought for their own safety. Even in a fenced yard, they should not be unattended while outdoors.

A dog belonging to the Toy group usually finds its way to the shelter or back to its original breeder because its owner didn't do his homework before acquiring the dog. The owner might have expected a quiet little lapdog instead of a lively, assertive little bundle of energy. Perhaps he found training too difficult and just gave up. These cute little dogs can have minds of their own!

Becaue many of the Toy breeds were originally bred as watch dogs, barking may be a problem. Make sure the people in neighboring apartments are "dog people" before bringing a brave little watch dog home. Toys can be trained out of barking at every strange footfall, but it will take time, patience and the advice of an experienced trainer. Also, check with your building manager about regulations governing pets.

There are 19 AKC-recognized Toy breeds from which to choose. They are the Affenpinscher, Brussels Griffon, Cavalier King Charles Spaniel, Chihuahua, Chinese Crested, English Toy Spaniel, Italian Greyhound, Japanese Chin, Maltese, Toy Manchester Terrier, Miniature Pinscher, Papillon, Pekingese, Pomeranian, Toy Poodle, Pug, Shih Tzu, Silky Terrier and Yorkshire Terrier.

A WIDE VARIETY

Dogs listed in the AKC Non-Sporting Group come from a variety of backgrounds and are good companions for people with various lifestyles and interests. As you research your breeds, you'll enjoy learning the history of each dog. One or two of these breeds may not be the most appropriate choice for a home with children or other pets; if you're interested, ask a breeder or fancier about this consideration. In general, though, dogs in this group make interesting, attractive and loyal pets.

The 16 Non-Sporting Dogs are: American Eskimo Dog, Bichon Frise, Boston Terrier, Bulldog, Chinese Shar-Pei, Chow Chow, Dalmatian, Finnish Spitz, French Bulldog, Keeshond, Lhasa Apso, Poodle, Schipperke, Shibu Inu, Tibetan Spaniel and Tibetan Terrier.

A LIFE OF SERVICE

Herding dogs deserve an experienced owner who is willing to devote sufficient time and energy to training and exercise. They're happiest when they have work to do. If they have no sheep or cattle to herd, they'll herd geese, chickens, other pets and even family members. At a Long Island, N.Y. obedience class, everyone laughed when a Border Collie nipped at a

No matter your pup's breed or background, you can ensure his health by feeding him a specially formulated food for puppies — one that is fortified with vitamin D and calcium to build strong teeth and bones, and that will fuel his high activity level with the proper nutrients. Photo courtesy of Cycle Dog Food.

In the right situation and with understanding and training, any type of dog can become the ideal family pet.

handler's ample behind to get her moving. He was following his instinct to organize the group of dogs and people into a herd.

Kipper, an English Springer Spaniel-Border Collie mix, tried to herd the family upstairs at bedtime. When the family started the going-to-bed routine: turning out lights, turning off the TV, putting down books and newspapers, she would trot from one family member to another, gently nudging each one with her nose, trotting behind to the bottom of the stairs. She would not settle down for the night until Mom, Dad and the two kids were all tucked in. Then she'd take her place at the top

of the stairs, guarding her family through the night. She had never been near a sheep, but the herding instinct bred into Border Collies for centuries surfaced in this suburban all-American, adopted as a pup.

Herding dogs enjoy agility, obedience and other competitive events that require intelligence, athletic ability and a keen memory for commands. They thrive on activity and are unhappy cooped up in the house. They pace, fret, and may become destructive. To satisfy your dog's instinct to work, and to have a great time yourself, consider enrolling in agility and obedience and agility classes.

The 16 Herding dogs recognized by the AKC are: Australian Cattle Dog, Australian Shepherd, Bearded Collie, Belgian Malinois, Belgian Sheepdog, Belgian Tervuren, Border Collie, Bouvier des Flandres, Briard, Collie, German Shepherd Dog, Old English Sheepdog, Puli, Shetland Sheepdog, Cardigan Welsh Corgi and Pembroke Welsh Corgi.

If after you've read everything you can get your hands on, attended dog shows and talked to veterinarians, breeders, friends and acquaintances, you still come across a breed you don't recognize, just ask the owner. Most people love to talk about their dogs.

With a visit to your local shelter you just might find a new best friend.

WHERE ARE ALL THE DOGS?

Cindy, a boisterous English Springer Spaniel, enjoyed outdoor activities with her owner Jim, who, at 84, enjoyed hiking and chopping wood for the fireplace. But one day, Cindy jumped on Jim's frail wife, knocking her to the floor. With tears in his eyes, Jim took Cindy to the shelter, hoping a young family with children would find her there.

Brandy, a friendly Labrador Retriever mix, turned not-so-friendly when the new baby arrived. Although he probably would have settled down in time, the inexperienced parents weren't willing to take the chance. They returned Brandy to the breeder from whom they had bought her.

Jerzy, a spotted all-American boy, was a great watch dog. Barking was his favorite activity. But when his owners moved into an apartment, they decided to give him up. Jerzy now attends training classes at a not-for-profit shelter and is getting ready for a new home.

If these dogs' owners had taken the time to teach their dogs acceptable behavior, they might still have them. But one person's sad ending is another's happy beginning. With love, attention and training, any of these dogs can have a new lease on life. You may be the one to provide it.

You might find your dog in another state at a breeder's kennel. Or he might be waiting patiently for you in a town shelter or private agency just down the road. You might even find the dog of your dreams in your own home as you surf the Internet on your computer.

THE LOCAL ANIMAL SHELTER

Rick, a tall, lanky artist, had

When you provide the love, attention and training, any dog can have a new lease on life.

never had a dog of his own. His family had dogs when he was growing up, but he had never really bonded with any of them—probably because it was his mom who fed them, walked them and stroked their heads. Rick heard through the local

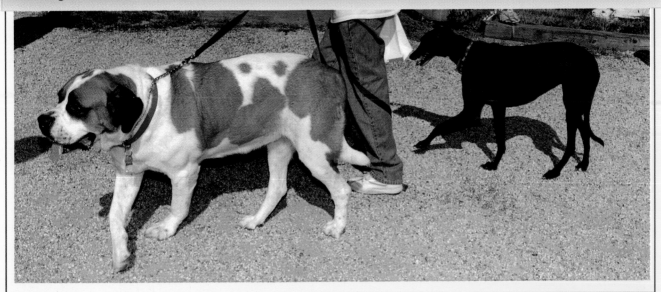

All dogs have different needs. Understanding the type of dog you may want to adopt can help keep a dog from returning to a shelter.

CD 20

HELP HOMELESS PETS

© 1996 HEINZ PET PRODUCTS

CYCLE®
DOG FOOD
Custom Fitness™

Help Homeless Pets
"I'm worth cash to your local animal shelter!"
For details call
1-800-842-4637
Program endorsed by the American Humane Association.

Make a difference in the lives of homeless animals in your community. Clip these Homeless Homer symbols from Cycle dog food, send them to your local American Humane Association or shelter, and Cycle will make a monetary donation to the shelter for every symbol they collect. Photo courtesy of Cycle Dog Food.

rescue network about a dog at the local shelter. The dog was big and difficult to handle. He needed a certain kind of person.

Rick went to see the dog. The large Golden Retriever mix had been at the shelter for a month, and was scheduled to be euthanized as soon as the shipment of chemicals arrived. Rick put his hand on the dog's broad golden head, and looked into the most beautiful, intelligent eyes he had ever seen.

He named the dog Arthur Pendragon Rabbit Boss. Arthur was a handful, but Rick was the right person to help him work off his energy. He was strong enough and firm enough to show Arthur that in Rick's house, Rick is the leader of the pack.

Now Rick and Arthur are like brothers. Every day they run together on the beach. They compete in agility matches. Arthur, the former shelter dog who cheated death,

has perfect manners. When Rick and Mei Ling were married, Arthur was their best man.

HOW THE SHELTER WORKS

Your town or county may have a public animal shelter (once known as a dog pound). Town or county shelters are supported by dog license fees, fines for violations of dog laws, grants and donations. Some shelters keep a dog for a limited time, during which they attempt to locate the owner if the dog was a stray or make the dog available for adoption if the owner has relinquished it to the shelter. If the dog is not adopted within that time, he may be moved to an adoption agency or a foster home to await adoption.

What kind of dog are you most likely to find in a shelter?

Your average shelter pooch is more likely to be an all-American mixed breed than a purebred dog.

He won't cost nearly as

much as a purebred dog you'd purchase from a breeder. Most shelters charge less than $100. Some include such extras as spaying or neutering, licensing, inoculations and ID—tags, tattoo or microchip—in that fee.

He's between one and two years old, or he's more than four years old. He's probably been neutered if a male or spayed if a female. Chances are, he'll need some training and maybe even some veterinary care. But if you're willing to meet him halfway, he'll come running the rest of the way to you. And he'll thank you for the rest of his life for giving him another chance.

A disadvantage, however, is that most dogs in a public shelter have no history. So be prepared to put in whatever time and expense may be necessary to treat health problems or eliminate bad habits such as constant barking, destructive chewing and digging, fear biting, agressiveness toward humans or other dogs, urination or defecation in the house, jumping or running away. One of these behaviors or all of the above may be what got the dog into the shelter in the first place. The last thing you want is to take your new pet on a return trip.

Proper training and discipline can help a dog avoid the shelter.

According to a survey, the main reason pets are left at the shelter is because their owners had underestimated the time they'd have to devote to their dogs' care and training. Hyperactivity, urinating and defecating in the house and unwanted chewing topped the list of behavioral problems in relinquished dogs.

"Mixed-breed dogs were 3.31 times more at risk than purebreds of being relinquished to shelters," the survey says. Staff members at several shelters corroborated this statement, saying that they house considerably more mixed breeds than purebred dogs.

Many owners prefer all-American pooches because they claim these dogs possess "hybrid vigor," the result of the blending of positive traits from a variety of breeds. All-American fanciers believe that the whole is greater than the sum of its parts; in other

One look at this dog tells you he is ready for you to take him home. Are you ready?

words, desirable canine features combine to create a new model dog with superior health, vigor, intelligence and structural soundness. Arthur is a fine example of this. But he was also an extremely dominant dog, and needed a special person to bring out his good qualities.

This study also found that dogs between one and two and more than four years old were most likely to be relinquished by their owners to shelters. If you've decided

This dog's expression says keen, alert and intelligent. Is he your type?

on a puppy, however, mention this to shelter personnel. Sometimes shelters in an area with a high demand for puppies will transport them from an area with an oversupply. Try to find out when the next group of puppies is due.

A VISIT TO THE SHELTER

When you enter the kennel area, walk slowly past all the dogs and take a good look at each one. Then narrow your

With blue eyes like this, this dog won't remain in the shelter for long. Others may not be so fortunate.

choice down to the ones you liked best. Walk past the dogs a second time, and a third, fourth, fifth if necessary, narrowing down your choice each time until you've decided on one dog. Don't take a dog home because you feel sorry for him, unless you are sure he is the right dog for you. Wait a week or so and visit the shelter again. You'll probably find that he has been adopted or moved to a foster home. And this time the dog you've been waiting for will be there.

If you handle a shelter dog, make sure a member of the staff assists you. Watch for aggressive behavior or cowardly, cringing behavior that might lead to fear biting. But keep in mind that a shelter dog will probably not act as he would in a familiar home. He is surrounded by strange smells and sights. He has been abandoned or has lost someone he loved and trusted. He may shiver and shake, or just sit and stare off into space. He may even snap and bite if he is unaccustomed to being handled by strangers. It is not his finest moment. When he has been in his new home for awhile and feels safe and loved, a delightful personality may blossom. If you see a dog you like, but you think he may have behavior problems, don't give up on him. Give him a chance.

SCHOOL FOR DOGS

In days long gone, a shelter was more or less a place to park a dog who eventually would leave through either the front or back door. In recent years, however, shelters have added activities that make their dogs more adoptable. Courses in many shelters' curricula are Training 101, Elementary, Intermediate and Advanced Socializing and Therapy Dog Prep School. Volunteers walk the dogs, train them to be good canine citizens and acclimate them to situations they may encounter with new owners — trips to town, socialization with other pets,

rides in the car, visits from strangers.

Also, in order to minimize the risk of adopted dogs bouncing right back to them, shelters have increased post-adoption assistance to new owners. They instruct them to take the dog to obedience training classes and to the veterinarian for regular visits.

Some shelters respond to the law of supply and demand by moving puppies and dogs from an overpopulated area to an area with a high demand for pets. For example, shelters in several southern states transport puppies by van to North Shore Animal League in Port Washington, New York, where families throughout the densely populated tri-state area eagerly anticipate the arrival of their new puppies. Last year North Shore rescued, transported and re-homed approximately 30,000 puppies from South Carolina, Virginia, Tennessee and the New York metropolitan area, according to a spokesperson for the shelter.

Safe and secure in his new home, a delightful personality will develop.

Probably the best-known shelter name is the American Society for the Prevention of Cruelty to Animals (ASPCA) in New York City, an organization that has cared for animals in need for 131 years. Its mission is to alleviate the pain, fear and suffering of all animals. Through its National Shelter Outreach Program, the ASPCA provides assistance, funding, advice and an occasional grant, according to a spokesperson.

NOT-FOR-PROFIT AGENCIES

These shelters often get the "overflow" from municipal shelters. Also, dogs are relinquished here directly by owners. These organizations are completely supported by grants and donations. They raise money through general appeal and special events such as pet parades, holiday parties, "alumni reunions" and community spay-and-neuter days in conjunction

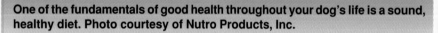

One of the fundamentals of good health throughout your dog's life is a sound, healthy diet. Photo courtesy of Nutro Products, Inc.

with a local veterinary clinic.

In addition to a small staff, an adoption agency depends on a large volunteer force to care for the animals and get them ready for adoption. Most agencies spay or neuter every dog, check for heartworm and other health problems and provide some inoculations (others must be administered by a veterinarian).

Not-for-profit shelters enhance a dog's chances for adoption by preparing him for his new life. Because most dogs are relinquished to shelters because of behavior problems, in-shelter training helps place well-behaved dogs and keep them in their new homes. For example, animal rescue and education center St. Hubert's Giralda in Madison, New Jersey, annually graduates 2,500 shelter dogs and dogs from the surrounding area from its pet training and competition

Puppies have a greater chance of being rescued. Looking at these three who could wonder why?

classes. Proceeds from the classes help support animals in the shelter. St. Hubert's outreach program educates children in responsible pet care. Each year, approx-imately 17,000 students who participate in St. Hubert's humane education program become more responsible potential dog owners.

Volunteers at the Animal Rescue Fund (ARF) of East Hampton, New York, pick up dogs at ARF headquarters and take them to town. The dogs become accustomed to riding in the car, walking along busy sidewalks and visiting homes. They learn to be good canine citizens. On Alumni Day, dogs at the shelter meet "graduates" who have been placed in loving, responsible homes. Some shelter dogs learn to be therapy dogs at nursing homes. If you'd like to do volunteer work in your community, you'd make a great contribution and have fun at the same time by adopting a therapy dog-in-training. After you finish training with him, you'll visit area hospitals and nursing homes.

You can often find a purebred in your local shelter. This is Gemma, a German Shepherd.

All perked up but nowhere to go, shelters provide a second chance for dogs like this.

dog. If the dog you want is purebred or an all-American that has the traits of a certain breed, ask agency personnel for information on that breed.

ADOPTING A PUREBRED DOG

There are several advantages to adopting a purebred dog. Breeders of purebred dogs are committed to maintaining and improving the breeds they love. Each breed has individual characteristics established through centuries of breeding. So when you've decided what characteristics you want in a dog, you know in which breeds you're likely to find them.

If a particular breed is susceptible to a hereditary disorder such as blindness, deafness or hip dysplasia, the breeders, through their national organizations in cooperation with veterinary colleges and organizations such as the AKC Canine Health Foundation and the Orthopedic Foundation for Animals (OFA), work toward eliminating the defect. They are concerned with the

ARF gets the entire community involved by holding fund-raising activities that are fun: The Parade of Pets, the Razzle-Dazzle Raffle and a Holiday Bazaar.

You can attend a fund-raiser to find out more about a shelter in your area and see dogs that are available for adoption. You might also want to pay a surprise visit to check out the facility. Does it smell clean? Are the dogs kept in comfortable cages? Are they let out frequently? Are dogs with suspected health problems quarantined from the others? Do shelter staff and volunteers take part in training and socializing the dogs?

You will probably be able to obtain more of a dog's history from the agency than from the public shelter. Ask about inoculations, behavior problems and past training.

Leave your name if the breed you want is not available. There are usually waiting lists for some of the most popular breeds, such as Labrador Retrievers, Golden Retrievers and Poodles. The shelter will notify you when they can match you with a

Purebred dogs, like this white German Shepherd, are often available at shelters, though you can also find them through purebred rescue.

welfare of the breed and of their individual dogs. They focus on breeding healthy dogs with good temperaments.

Purebred dogs, with health certificates and pedigrees going back several generations, can be expensive. But sometimes a purebred dog or puppy becomes available for adoption at minimal cost. For example, a reputable breeder always will take back a dog that has been returned to him or her because the new owner has not found the dog suitable. Perhaps the owner found the dog difficult to housetrain. Or he had not researched the breed before purchasing and decided after a few days, weeks or months that this was not the breed for him. Or the dog did not fit in with other animals in the household. Or he chewed up his favorite shoes. Or had an "accident" on the new carpet. For whatever reason, the pup ends up back at the breeder's. And that's where you come in.

Reputable breeders believe that they are responsible for puppies that they have brought into the world. Although it rarely is convenient for them to find new homes for their dogs after they have sold them, they will sometimes place them in adoptive homes with people

All dogs are individuals. Find one to suit your personality and activity level.

Even purebreds become available for adoption. Check with your local shelter to see if a certain breed is available.

they determine will be responsible owners.

If the breeder hasn't yet had the dog neutered or spayed, she will ask you to sign a spay-neuter contract, agreeing that within a certain number of days you will have this procedure carried out by a veterinarian. All pet dogs should be spayed or neutered. Anyone who is not a serious breeder is seriously irresponsible if he brings puppies into a world already populated by millions of adoptable dogs.

The breeder will also ask you to sign an agreement stating that the dog will be examined by your veterinarian within 48 hours of adoption. (No matter where you get your dog, this is an excellent idea.)

When you visit a breeder, you can see other dogs of the same breed and how they

interact with one another, the breeder and you. Are they playful? Shy? Rough-and-tumble? Too strong? Skittish? Affectionate? Is your potential best friend dominant or submissive with other dogs and with people? You may even be able to see the parents of the dog you're about to adopt.

You'll also have the opportunity to talk with the breeder and learn more about the breed and the individual dog. Did unfortunate circumstances lead to the dog's return? Are there learned behaviors you'll have to train him out of?

If you are interested in adopting a purebred dog, contact the national club for that breed. National breed clubs have names like United States Lakeland Terrier Club, Tibetan Spaniel Club of America and Collie Club of

There is a huge network of people working to rehome dogs, and celebrating when they do. This is Buddy, enjoying himself at the Parade of Pets Shelter fundraiser.

company cafeteria asking for volunteers to fly with the rescued dogs to their new homes. He happened to be involved in rescuing dogs himself, so he picked up the phone and called Gordon Bethune, Continental's Chief Executive Officer. Bethune, a dog lover, agreed not only to help, but to fly all 68 dogs anywhere in the US.

National breed clubs can put you in touch with their network of rescue volunteers. In a way, the breeder-rescue network is an extended family, concerned with the welfare of all dogs.

If you know a veterinarian, ask if he or she knows of any nice, adoptable dogs. Often veterinarians form relationships with purebred rescue organizations and can even direct you to the breed you're looking for.

An active advocate of purebred rescue is National Animal Interest Alliance (NAIA), a national non-profit animal welfare organization. Each year representatives from some of the 2,000 rescue groups all over the US attend an NAIA symposium that honors shelter personnel and purebred rescue advocates and features presentations by leading veterinarians, behaviorists, trainers, attorneys, breeders, AKC officials and individuals involved in rescue on national, state and local levels.

Another organization that coordinates efforts with breed clubs throughout the country is All-Breed Rescue Alliance, Inc. (ABRA). You can find the addresses for the NAIA and ABRA at the end of this book.

How do the approximately

America. The AKC has a list of clubs' addresses and phone numbers.

The national club will put you in touch with a breed club in your area. Let the local club know that you are intererested in adopting a dog of their breed. If a breeder in the club is looking for a good home for one of his or her puppies or adult dogs, the club will give him your name and he will contact you.

ADOPTION THROUGH PUREBRED RESCUE

Dogs flew to new homes across the country when Alaskan Malamute Rescue (AMR) of South Texas, in a cooperative effort with AMR of Michigan and AMR of Ohio, rescued 68 Mals. It was the largest-ever rescue of that breed, according to Susan Ingersoll-Cloer, founder of the Texas group.

An employee of Continental Airlines saw a notice in the

2,000 rescue organizations across the country work? Some are nationally organized with full breed club support. Others are coordinated by regional clubs or groups of individuals interested in helping a particular breed or breeds. Rescue workers develop relationships with animal control agencies and shelters, that contact them if an animal of their breed is relinquished by its owner or picked up as a stray. The breed club supplies shelter staff members and volunteers with literature, including illustrations and photos, so that when a dog of that breed comes into the shelter, they can identify it and notify a club member, who will pick the dog up.

Rescue workers also educate shelter personnel about characteristics of their breed. The importance of this service was emphasized by a rescue worker who was called to a shelter to pick up several dogs of a particular breed that had been left there. When she arrived, a shelter staff

Hailey and Paco are just two examples of how mixed breeds make wonderful pets.

This mix, Dorothy, is another canine success story, shown here clearing an agility jump.

member told her that three of the six dogs had been euthanized because they were "hyper." They had charged at the fence and barked whenever anyone came near. The three who had been saved were timid, trembling, quiet little things — not at all typical of the breed. If the shelter workers had known that this particular breed is supposed to be active, assertive and very lively, they would have acted differently. It was a sobering lesson for the rescue volunteers, who increased their efforts to educate shelter personnel about their breed.

Once rescue volunteers have been notified, the next step is to make every effort to locate the breeder of the dog, who should take back the dog and place it with a responsible owner. If the breeder cannot be found, or if the dog is from someone or someplace that takes no

interest in the pups once they're sold, the rescue worker usually places the dog with a foster home where it is cared for, evaluated for temperament and behavorial tendencies and taken to the vet for a checkup, shots and treatment if needed.

Advantages in adopting from a purebred rescue organization are that the dog has been screened for health problems, inoculated and spayed or neutered. Each dog is evaluated for temperament, so that any behavioral problems can be quickly identified.

Sometimes the new owner is asked to absorb the cost of surgical sterilization or make a donation to the group, which may also raise funds through special events such as community spay-neuter days, pet parades or pet photos-with-Santa sessions. Sometimes, too, a veterinarian will perform the procedure as

Her owners call her "Graffitti" because she's "freckled and speckled and then some."

purebred rescue volunteer, don't be put off by the questions he or she asks you. She's not being nosy or uppity; she just wants to make sure her dog goes to a home where he will be appreciated, properly cared for, respected and loved. The rescue organization will also ask you to fill out an application and questionnaire. Some of the questions you'll be asked are:

Have you ever had a dog before?

What breeds have you had?

Do you have a dog now?

Do you have any other pets?

What happened to your previous dog(s)?

Why are you interested in this breed?

Have you ever had a dog of this breed?

What do you know about this breed?

Do you have children? What are their ages?

What kind of house/

a service in return for referrals, or simply because he or she loves dogs.

Each rescue group forms a policy about injured or ill dogs. Will they make the extra effort to place these dogs or have them mercifully euthanized so that more healthy dogs will have a chance at a new lease on life? If you have the temperament and inclination to give an old dog comfort and love in his last days, or nurse an injured or ill dog back to health, speak up. You'll have plenty of company, because others like you have discovered that not only is caring for an older dog a reward in itself, but that the love and companionship an older dog can give is immeasurable.

BE PREPARED FOR A QUIZ

As rescue workers and foster families evaluate dogs,

interviewers evaluate potential new owners and endeavor to match each dog with the right owner.

When you visit a breeder or

Rescue workers will ask many questions to match the best dog for your lifestyle.

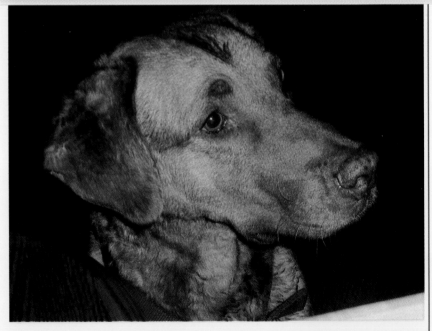

apartment do you have? What is its size?

Do you live in a rural, suburban or urban area?

Is your yard fenced?

Will you agree to a home-check by a breeder or rescue organization?

Will the dog be alone during the day?

Does anyone in your family have allergies?

What is your activity level?

Will you train the dog in obedience?

Do you travel often? What provisions would be made for the dog?

Do you prefer male or female?

What size dog do you want?

What kind of coat do you want? Can you put time and money into grooming or do you prefer a "maintenance-free" coat?

Would you adopt a dog who has health problems?

Would you adopt an elderly dog? A puppy?

How long are you willing to wait for a dog?

Will you return the dog to this rescue organization if you can no longer care for him?

Being loved and cared for, his only concern now is his water bowl.

Maybe the best ride of your life will be the ride home with your newly adopted friend.

When you submit the completed form, you'll also send a small fee, usually less than $10, to cover processing.

Now it's your turn to ask some questions. Request an information packet from the breeder or rescue agency. A reputable breeder or organization will have assembled for potential adopters:

Breed history

Health care booklets and articles

Training tips and articles

Names and addresses of local trainers

Rescue group brochure

Health and immunization record

Nutritional information and feeding recommendations

Health problems associated with breed.

Ask the breeder or rescuer:

Why is the dog available for adoption?

Does he have any bad habits?

Has he ever bitten a person or another dog?

Is he housetrained?

Is he trained to the leash?

Has he had any formal training?

Where has he slept? On the bed? In a crate? Outdoors?

Is he good with children?

Does he have favorite toys?

How does he act with strangers? Other pets? Visitors to the house?

How much exercise does he need?

When can I pick him up?

Write down these any any other questions you'd like to ask, just in case every thought flies out of your head when a cute little guy with a wagging tail pounces on you and covers your face with wet kisses.

Rescue dogs come in all shapes and sizes. Search diligently to find the right dog for you.

DOGS.COM: RESCUE ON THE INTERNET

Imagine dogs of all shapes, colors and sizes flying Toto-like through cyberspace to land in good homes, and you'll have a picture of today's dog rescue communications on the Internet/World Wide Web. For these relocated dogs, there's no place like home—homes found through clicking keyboards, updated versions of Dorothy's magical ruby slippers in *The Wizard of Oz*.

Here's an example of one lucky dog and one very persistent human who were brought together by the Internet. They are a Chesapeake Bay Retriever and Dave, a man looking for a Chessie. He put a message on the 'Net, and covered all bases by visiting shelters near his Fairfield, California home. He heard about a Chessie named Barney at a shelter and went to have a look. When he got there, he was told that the dog had been euthanized because he was a biter.

A woman who had seen Dave's message on the 'Net called him to say, "That dog Barney is still there! They didn't euthanize him!"

Dave drove back to the shelter. The dog, a nice Chessie, was in quarantine. Shelter workers told Dave he had bared his teeth at the veterinarian who had examined him.

It took all afternoon to convince shelter officials, but finally Dave was permitted to take Barney. As he approached his car in the shelter parking lot, a worker came up to him and told him that they had attempted to put Barney down, but he had tried to bite them. They had been waiting for help in holding him when Dave arrived at the shelter.

"He turned out to be a wonderful dog," says Dave. The bared teeth hadn't been an indication that Barney was a fear biter, after all. It was just a "Chessie smile," and because Dave had been familiar with the breed, he saw this as a possibility and saved Barney's life.

A "Chessie smile" is just that. Dave reports that Barney smiles whenever he is anxious. "When he's ready to

Dogs communicate in many ways, and their body language can tell you a lot about their personalities.

This Lab-Collie mix is all smiles at the prospect of finding a new home.

most traveled are CompuServe, America Online, Prodigy, Worldnet and various Internet providers with local or 800 numbers.

In addition to 'Net access and e-mail capability, CompuServe and America Online provide "bulletin boards" where you can exchange messages, view descriptions and download photos. Click. You move from the messages section to the library. Click. You're into the rescue section, where you'll find an electronic storehouse of articles and art on rescue topics. Some recent offerings include "All-Breed Rescue Contacts and Shelters," "National Breed Club Rescue Contacts," "Saving More Lives," "Fostering Dogs"—just a small sample of material you have access to without leaving the house. The on-line services also offer breed chat rooms or forums scheduled for certain times each week when rescuers around the world chat with prospective dog owners by simultaneously sending messages via their keyboards.

As you follow the ever-branching road through the

go for a walk and when it's dinnertime, he smiles. When something he's not used to happens, he smiles."

Maybe Barney smiles so much because Dave happened to come along just in the nick of time.

BULLDOGS AND BULLETIN BOARDS

"Within five years the Internet will take the place of all other means of communication in rescue," predicts Kathy DeWees of All-Breed Rescue Alliance (ABRA)

and Delaware Valley Akita Rescue. "Fully one-half the inquiries I get come from the Web. On some days I get 200 e-mail messages."

"On our listings of dogs available for adoption, photos are a big help," DeWees says. With a few clicks, a prospective owner can view photos of dogs available for adoption.

In locating a beautiful purebred dog who needs a responsible, loving owner, all roads lead to the information superhighway. The routes

Sometimes the best present can be a second chance.

Whether it's by the information superhighway known as the World Wide Web, or by word of mouth, rescue workers are letting the world know there are plenty of good dogs available.

Web, here are some stops you'll make on the way to adopting a dog: **http://www. akc.org** is the AKC web site from which you can access information about adopting a purebred dog by clicking on a hyperlink of the breed name. (A hyperlink is an underlined word or words describing the topic you're searching for. When your cursor passes over a hyperlink, it is transformed into a little hand with an extended index finger clicking on a hyperlink will transport you to a place within that web site, or perhaps to another web site, that will give you furthur information on the topic you've selected.) **http:// www.akc.org/akc/car.htm** is Companion Animal Recovery. It provides information about the AKC program for finding lost dogs that carry positive identification on a microchip which can be read by rescue workers using a scanner. Some shelters provide microchip ID when you adopt

a dog from them. **http://www. pro.dogs.com** is a web site offering information on breeders, canine health and other dog-related topics. Half of its pages are dedicated to rescue; page set-up and listings are free to rescue groups. **http://www. rec.pet.dogs.rescue** can be accessed from all the major on-line computer services. It is a newsgroup where members can exchange information and receive *The Complete List of Dog Related E-Mail Lists*, which is updated every two weeks. This is an extensive list of publicly available dog-related e-mail lists, including breed-specific lists and Rescue lists. **http://www .canismajor.com.naia/** is NAIA (National Animal Interest Alliance), the resource and support group for rescue, where you'll find information on purebred rescue. **http:// www.azstarnet.com/~labsal/ mwhome.htm** will get you to

the Midwest Animal Shelter, a no-kill shelter that flies dogs all over the country to approved homes.

It's like a big, friendly, wagging, whole new world out there on the information superhighway. The Sheltie people help the Aussie people, Pom people send Spaniel surfers over to the right breed home page, Skip fancier meets Skip, and all-American mutts of every variety fly from state to state.

It's quite a place, and well worth a visit. Bet you won't stop with just one!

A word of warning: Most individuals you'll encounter in Internet rescue are honest, dedicated dog lovers. However, where there's money to be made, unscrupulous individuals will gather and the Internet is no exception. If you see a listing that sounds suspicious, notify one of the rescue support groups.

A dog doesn't have much in common with a computer, but it is possible to use the latter to find the former.

All dogs love a soft warm spot - like a lap - to curl up in. Make sure you provide at least one such spot in your home.

BRINGING BABY HOME

Before you bring your puppy or dog home, get the house ready. This is an exciting time, and the whole family can take part in selecting new items that will give your dog a sense of belonging. Most of these supplies can be found in your local pet supply store, where staff members can answer any questions you may have.

A GOOD-QUALITY CRATE

All dogs need a special place they can call their own. Your dog will come to regard his crate as a haven of safety where he can nap undisturbed. He'll go directly to his crate when it's time to take him on a car trip.

Sometimes he'll go to his crate when he just wants to be alone. And crate training can be an effective method of teaching your new dog good manners from day one.

The crate should be big enough for the dog to stand and move around in, but small enough that he will feel snug and secure. For the bottom of the crate, get a tray that you can slide out for cleaning. Cover it with a comfy pad made of lambswool or some other soft, warm fabric that you can throw in the washing machine. Add a dog cushion and small blanket. Food and water dishes that fasten to the bars of the crate are a handy

addition. As a welcome-home present, throw in a nice Carrot Bone™ or Roar-Hide™ chew for him to munch on.

If you're planning to paper train your dog, stock up on newspapers. Let your friends and aquaintances know you'd appreciate a donation of piles of newspapers.

A DOG BED

Your dog's bed should be made of a soft, comfortable, washable fabric stuffed with washable filling or with cedar chips that can be changed when the bed is washed. When he first comes home, your dog will feel secure if you allow him to sleep in or near your bedroom. Dogs like to

The whole family can get involved with getting the house and yard ready for the arrival of the new family dog.

Outdoors or in, your new dog will need plenty of exercise—especially if he's a large, active breed.

feel a solid surface at their backs, so put the bed in a corner or against a wall. Most trainers advise against letting your dog sleep on your bed. They say this makes the dog think he is on an equal or even higher level than his humans, and will make training difficult.

Some dogs really appreciate it when their owners pull their beds outdoors in warm weather, so they can bask in the sun in comfort.

FOOD AND WATER DISHES

Small, medium or large, the size of the dish should match the size of the dog. Stainless steel or heavy ceramic dishes are best. Put them in the kitchen or an enclosed porch, so your dog will always know where to go for food and water. Freshen the water every day, and check frequently in hot weather to see if the water dish needs refilling.

Have some fun. Order a special dish with your dog's name on it. You can find a good selection of dishes ranging in price from less than $5 to over $50! But not everyone thinks his dog can't live without a crystal dish with a silver nameplate.

SPEAKING OF NAMES

You may decide to call your new dog by his old name. But why not start fresh? Discuss various names before you get the dog, but don't make a final decision until he has been home for a few days. The way he acts or looks may give you a clue. Examples are Boomer, Sport, Baby, Mitey, Spike, Panda or Honcho. Many owners like to give their dogs contemporary human names such as Molly, Arthur, Lucy, Fred and Jimmy, or classic monikers such as Brutus, Zeus, Helen and Cato. It's a good idea to give a dog a short, snappy name with a vowel at the end, so

When deciding on a name, maybe the way he looks or acts will give you a clue.

that when you call him, you can give a pleasant-sounding upward inflection at the end: "Jimm-ee, come!"

Maybe your dog will tell you his name. Watch carefully. Listen to what he tells you by expression and action.

Then use the name constantly when talking to your dog. Say it over and over while petting and stroking him. Say it to get his attention before starting a new activity: "Sandy, time for dinner!"

"Sandy, time to go out!" "Gooood Sandy."

COLLAR AND LEASH

These items should be in the car and ready for your first (and maybe only) trip to the shelter or breeder. Have them ready to put on your dog before you leave the shelter. Hold them out to him and let him sniff them. Then gently put them on and stand still for a minute while the dog becomes accustomed to the feel of them. Keeping your eyes on your dog, start for the car while talking to him gently. This is when your dog might decide to make a break for it. Hold on!

Of course, if you've just adopted a puppy, the rules are different. Put the collar and leash on and then carry him out to the car. You'll have plenty of time to get him used to collar and leash at home.

Also get a training collar (commonly called a choke chain). You'll use this in teaching your dog to walk with you without pulling, and in various obedience commands. Never use this kind of collar on a puppy less than six months old.

Accustom your new dog to his collar and leash as soon as you get him.

Rambone's favorite toy of all is his tennis ball, even though he has other chew toys to pass his time.

Safe squeaky toys are another favorite, as are old tennis balls, Gumarings™ and Gumaknots™.

NAIL CARE TOOLS

Use your dog's clippers once a week or clip nails short soon after he arrives home, and keep them short and neat by regular grinding. Some dogs object to having their nails done, so introduce these objects carefully, a little at a time. First, allow your dog to sniff the clippers while you talk to him soothingly. (Don't overdo the soothing part, though, because most dogs quickly pick up that sweet talking from a human means that something unpleasant is certain to follow.) Next day, touch the toenails. Third day, clip.

Trim your dog's nails on a regular schedule. This routine keeps nails from catching on objects, including your favorite sweater. It also

CHEW TOYS

A problem behavior often associated with adopted dogs is inappropriate chewing; in other words, mistaking the sofa, your shoe or table legs for dinner. Toys that promote healthy chewing, such as Nylabones®, Gumabones® and Puppybones®, will exercise your dog's jaws, help keep his teeth clean and make him forget all about your slippers.

Another treat, especially in summer, is a sterilized femur bone stuffed with peanut butter and then placed in your freezer. This will keep your dog busy for hours as he concentrates on getting to the peanut butter. Don't leave the bone outdoors, however, or it will fill up with ants.

When it's important to know what's in the products you use on your dog, it's nice to know there are foods and grooming aids made of the highest quality ingredients. Photo courtesy of Noah's Kingdom. For the location of a dealer near you call 1-800-662-4711.

Something to sing about: This dog lets everyone know he just found a new home.

prevents nails from tearing when the dog is running or digging outdoors. Overgrown nails often cause the toes to splay or spread out, ruining the shape of the dog's foot.

IDENTIFICATION

When you adopt, some shelters include in their fee a valuable item—ID for your dog. You may get a form to send in for a set of tags engraved with your dog's name and phone number, or you may receive tags at the shelter. Attach these to your dog's collar immediately.

Also, when you take your dog to the veterinarian for his post-adoption examination, ask him or her about tattooing and microchipping, two methods of canine ID.

Some veterinarians apply ID numbers in a permanent

Mr. Higgins plants a big kiss on his best friend, Mugsy. Both dogs were adopted by Jean Mitchell.

tattoo, usually inside your dog's thigh. The procedure is also done at dog shows, where you can have your dog

tattooed free of charge or for a small contribution. While you hold your dog, talking to him and reassuring him, a qualified person administers the tattoo. The dog feels a slight pricking sensation.

Microchipping is the latest development in canine ID. The system consists of a tiny microchip with your dog's ID number , which is registered in a national database; a scanner that can read the ID number on the microchip; and an 800 number imprinted on the scanner and on your dog's collar tag.

A veterinarian implants the microchip, the size of a grain of rice, just under the dog's skin between his shoulders. The implantation needle causes the dog about as much discomfort as a simple immunization shot. The chip cannot move around inside the dog because it is coated with a material that adheres to the dog's tissue at the spot of implantation. It is encased in biocompatible glass, so the

No chance of these dogs getting lost—their ID's are clear even from a distance!

dog's body does not reject it. Microchipping costs about $10.

A database is maintained by the AKC Companion Animal Recovery Program. When a lost dog is found, the organization is contacted through the 800 number on the dog's tag, and the AKC will instruct the finder to take the dog to the nearest location where a scanner reading can establish positive identification of the animal. If a dog has lost its collar and tag, the scanner can determine if the animal has been microchipped. A new

It only takes a minute for your dog or puppy to get lost—and yet it only takes a minute or so to get an I.D. tag that will protect your dog from being lost permanently. Protect your pet with the most visible identification system available: a tag. Photo courtesy of Quick Tag; for the location of the Quick Tag Engraving System machine nearest you, call 1-888-600 -TAGS.

ID tags are a must for your adopted dog. They can help return your pet in case you become separated.

universal scanner that can read all brands of microchips regardless of manufacturer virtually guarantees recovery of all animals registered in the AKC program.

After scanning, the vet or shelter employee reports the dog's ID number to the Companion Animal Recovery program, which, in turn, tells the owner where the animal is being held, and notifies the vet or shelter personnel that the owner has been contacted. A follow-up call is placed to the owner within 48 hours to ascertain that the owner and dog have been reunited. Your veterinarian can tell you more about the program, or call AKC Companion Animal Recovery at (800) 252-7894.

The importance of ID-ing your dog immediately can't be overemphasized. Every dog's middle name is Houdini.

Despite your best efforts, your dog may slip out one day and be picked up by the animal control officer. If your dog carries ID, you'll be notified and can pick him up. If he doesn't, anything could happen.

GROOMING AIDS

Take time in advance to shop for good grooming equipment, so you can start a routine shortly after you bring your new friend home. Choose a brush or grooming mitt that will keep your dog's coat neat, whatever its length. Also get a metal flea comb you can use to check your dog's coat for these pests. Doggy shampoo, liquid spot and odor remover and a few extra rolls of paper towels should round out the dog shelf in your broom closet.

When you call your vet-erinarian for an appointment

within 48 hours after you pick up your dog, ask him or her about flea and tick treatments that are safe and effective for your dog.

DOG-PROOF YOUR HOME

There's a TV commercial in which a puppy grabs one end of the toilet paper and runs through the house unrolling the long white streamer behind him. It really happens! And that's one of the mildest antics pups and older dogs can get into. Your dog's natural curiosity will get him into trouble and could even kill him. You must protect him.

Before visiting the shelter or kennel, dog-proof your home. Set aside a room or crate where the dog can stay safely when you are out of the house. In the rest of the house, put breakable or chewable items out of reach as much as possible. Remove potential hazards such as household cleaning supplies, insecticides, rodent poisons, mothballs, matchbooks, medications and household plants—some of which are poisonous.

Tell family members to keep toilet lids down. Keep pens,

A dog's nose can certainly lead him into trouble. Dog-proof your house before you bring your adopted dog home.

pencils, sewing supplies, balloons, rubber bands and plastic bags under cover. Place chicken and turkey bones and metal cans with ragged edges directly in a garbage can with a tight-fitting lid.

Electrical cords are a chewing attraction. If your dog has enough chew toys such as Nylabone® and Gumabone® Wishbone®, he may lose interest in attacking electric cords and cables. Also, ask your veterinarian or pet supply store staff member about bitter-tasting products you can apply to electric cords.

Be especially careful not to leave antifreeze where you dog can get it. It tastes sweet to dogs, and it is lethal.

Make sure your fence is adequate. A fence should be

It's up to you to safeguard your dog. Training helps. Biz is doing his "stay" on the table on an agility course.

Most Nylabone® products—like the Carrot Bone™—provide the necessary resistance to facilitate good jaw exercise in your dog.

at least five feet high for small and medium dogs and at least six feet high for large dogs. It should be sunk into concrete or the bottom edged with concrete blocks or stones. If you take these precautions, an extremely smart dog might soon realize digging is futile. Most dogs, however, will keep trying.

If you have a garden, check your plants or shrubs to make sure none are poisonous. Your library or local garden club can provide you with a list of toxic plants in your region.

Pools can be dangerous to dogs. If you have a pool, make sure someone is always in the vicinity when your dog is in the yard. If your dog decides to take a dip, he's going to try to get out, and might exhaust himself trying to clamber up the slippery side. Teach him to swim to the shallow end and climb up the steps. Invest in the kind of pool cover that locks in place. If your dog runs across it, it bouces back like a trampoline. The loose plastic covers are dangerous,

because your dog can fall in and become snagged beneath the cover.

If someone is treating the pool with chemicals, keep your animals inside the house until all chemical containers have been removed from the area.

HOMEWARD BOUND

Best time to bring your dog home: At the beginning of a vacation or long weekend, when family members—and no one else—will be there.

Worst time to bring a dog home: The Christmas holidays.

Year after year, people continue to give dogs and puppies as Christmas presents. It is the worst—repeat, worst—time to introduce a dog into new surroundings.

Nothing in the home is as it is the rest of the year. Tensions run high, strange people come and go. The sensual overload of noise, smells, bright lights and constant motion must make a dog's head spin. Danger is

everywhere: Poinsettias and mistletoe, both of which are poisonous, are the favorite plants of the season. Humans with too much eggnog under their belts act in strange, un-predictable ways.

The dog is not walked on schedule and relieves himself in the house. Gifts are left under the tree and are chewed to bits. Uncle Ralph lunges at the cute new dog for a kiss and gets a bite instead. The dog's new family feeds him too much turkey and he has diarrhea all over the house. He eats a five-pound bag of hard candy and throws up.

Awaiting adoption at the Quincy Humane Society. "Hey, care to join me for a drink."

The holidays come and go. What seemed like a good idea at the time is now reevaluated in light of the new dog's inability to adjust. It's back to the shelter.

Don't do this to an innocent dog. Choose a time when he can come home to a quiet, serene environment. Allow him to become accustomed to family members before introducing relatives and friends into the mix. By Christmas he'll fit right in.

FITTING IN

Your new dog has been abandoned once, and is afraid. He wants to keep you within sight all the time. He'll be your shadow as you get to know each other and he begins to feel comfortable with you. But sometimes you'll have to leave the house and he'll be alone for a while. He needs to know that some things are his own—his dishes, his bed, his toys, a

Your new dog will want to keep you in his sight at all time. Make him as comfortable as possible in his new surroundings.

Keep a close eye on your new dog as he settles into his new home and surroundings. Praise him when he does something right.

place where he feels snug and secure while you're gone.

On the first day, show him his crate and encourage him to enter it. If he's reluctant, throw a POPpup® chicken-or-liver-flavor edible bone in there to tempt him. Keep the crate in an area where he can watch the family. Put it against a wall. Dogs like to have something behind them when they settle down. Afer a while he'll enter the crate on his own so he can have an undisturbed nap.

At first leave the crate door open so he can come and go as he likes. After a few days, close the door when he goes inside. Leave the room for a few minutes. Come back and unlatch the door. Repeat this, leaving him in the crate for longer periods of time. When

you have to go out, he'll be comfortable in his "den" until you return, and you won't worry that he'll get into mischief while you're gone.

Don't leave your dog in his crate for extended periods of time. Crates should be used for short-term confinement, house training and travel. But no dog is happy cooped up all day in a small area. If no one is home during the day, leave him in a dog-proof area of the house and arrange for one family member or a neighbor he knows and trusts to check on him during the day, play with him and take him out. Leave the radio on a classical music station to soothe him until you come home.

Don't make leaving and returning a major production. Greet him when you come in, but don't act as if you haven't

If no one is home during the day, leave your dog in a safe area of the house and arrange for a friend to check on him.

seen him for weeks. He'll soon settle in and adapt to your routine. If a great deal of excitement surrounds your leaving and returning, he might develop separation anxiety, which manifests itself in destructive behavior such as chewing furniture, digging and scratching, incessant howling and barking, or urinating and defecating in the house.

While your dog is getting used to his new home, keep an eye on him. Watch everything he does. When he does something right, praise him. When he does something wrong, correct him. There's no need to shout and carry on. When you praise good behavior, use your dog's name. When you correct inappropriate behavior, never

Cinders knows he's being a good boy for laying down and staying while his picture is being taken.

use the name. Dogs are sensitive. You want to begin your life together by

associating his name with all good things, not something unpleasant.

Introduce all new objects and changes in routine gradually and calmly.

WHEN YOU ALREADY HAVE A DOG

You can't prepare your other dogs for the blessed event by telling them they're going to have a new little brother or sister. But you can plan ahead to prevent a fiasco when you introduce the new pack member.

Consider sexual characteristics. Pet dogs you already have should be spayed or neutered, as should any new dogs you bring into the family. This eliminates the sort of aggressive behavior two bitches (intact female dogs) or two intact males will display toward each other. And, of course, there won't be any backyard breeding adding to the misery of too many dogs and too few homes.

Your adult dog needs a food that will help him convert fuel to energy and supply him with the nutrients he needs for overall good health. Photo courtesy of Cycle Dog Food.

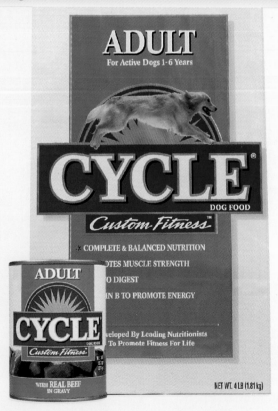

Spaying or neutering your all-American dog will help control the pet population problem.

All other things being equal, neutered dogs will get along with each other. However, some dogs are dominant and others are submissive. In adopting a dog, try to select one whose personality will complement that of the dog you already have. Try to find out at the shelter or from the breeder or rescue person if the dog has a history of aggression or dominance. It is not fair to the dog you already have to bring in a dog that will knock him from his rightful place in the pack. It would be better to introduce a less dominant but not overly submissive dog.

Try to arrange the dogs' first meeting outdoors, in a neutral setting. Walk your new dog down the street and meet another family member walking your other dog. Let the dogs sniff, get acquainted and decide what they want to do about this new situation. Walk along together for awhile. When you get home, let them romp in the fenced yard. They'll quickly establish pack order. There may be a few skirmishes from time to time, but if you've selected thoughtfully, two neutered dogs should be pals.

When you give the new dog a toy, give the other dog one, too. While you show the new dog his bed, his crate and his other belongings, and while you begin training him, have someone keep the settled family dog somewhere else. The two dogs will be rivals for your affections, so give each time alone with you— walks, rides in the car, quiet times—especially in the first few weeks.

Like people, dogs have different nutritional needs at different life stages. Consult with your veterinarian to identify those stages, and feed an appropriate diet for your dog's age or lifestyle. Photo courtesy of Cycle Dog Food.

THE HEALTHY DOG

FEEDING YOUR NEW DOG

Your dog has been through one stressful change after another, so don't add to his stress by introducing a new diet at this time. Find out what he has been fed at the shelter or breeder's, and give him the same thing after he comes home. If you decide to change food, do it over a week, gradually decreasing the amount of his previous brand and adding a little of the new brand each time.

If you have adopted a puppy, don't give him any milk. He has been weaned by the time he is ready for adoption, and milk at this stage will only cause gastric distress. Provide plenty of fresh water. As you housebreak him, you may want to give him water only at mealtimes.

Also, ask your veterinarian about supplemental vitamins for your puppy.

Try feeding your puppy small amounts of food formulated for puppies, several times a day. If he eats only part of a meal or no food at all, take him to the vet imediately. Loss of appetite in a pup is an indication of life-threatening illness such as parvovirus or coronavirus.

When your puppy is between four and six months old, reduce feedings to two or three times a day. If the puppy walks away from his food, pick up his dish until his next scheduled feeding time. This will train him to eat on schedule. Ask your veterinarian whether you should stay with the same puppy food or change to another formula at this time.

From six months on, give your dog two feedings a day. As your pup becomes an adult, maintain a balanced diet according to his level of activity. Check with your veterinarian about matching the composition of your dog's food to his lifestyle.

GROOMING

When you groom your dog regularly, you'll help her look her best, strengthen the bond between you and keep her healthy. Pay attention to her coat, teeth, eyes, ears and nails. Go through the coat for burrs, fleas and ticks. Brush the long coat, and stroke a grooming mitt over the short coat. Look for dry skin, irritations and scabs.

Many mixed breeds excel at agility work. Always praise your dog for a job well done.

It is best to feed your new pup the same food he was eating before you brought him home. Any change in diet should be made gradually.

Some dogs need to be bathed only once or twice a year. Others, especially dogs who like the great outdoors and tend to pick up mud and roll in various foul-smelling things, will need more frequent baths. Use a shampoo formulated for dogs.

Clean your dog's outer ears once a week. If there is unusual odor or secretion, or if your dog shakes his head and digs at his ears, infection might be present. Ask your veterinarian to have a look.

Eyes should be clear. If there is tearing under the eyes, wipe the area with a damp washcloth. Make sure eyelashes or hairs do not rub against the eyeball.

Check your dog's mouth for sores, bad breath and tartar formation. Introduce a canine toothbrush and toothpaste. Regular cleaning of his teeth should help retard the formation of plaque. Also beneficial in preventing plaque and calculus build-up are Plaque Attackers® and Galileo Bones®. As he chews

If your dog needs help staying fit or maintaining his ideal weight, it's wise to feed him a diet that's lower in fat and has fewer calories, yet still provides complete and balanced nutrition. Photo courtesy of Cycle Dog Food.

Ears should be checked for mites and other problems regularly.

on them, the solid polyurethane massages the gums, improving circulation. The projections on the surface of the chew toys brush against the teeth, helping to keep them clean.

If your dog's nails click on the floor, they're too long. Trim them once a week with clippers. Be careful not to cut into the quick. This hurts the dog, who won't be eager to cooperate with you the next time. If your adopted dog's nails are too long when he comes home, just cut off a little at first, then a little more, until they're close to the foot. Then keep them short by using a grinder every other day.

FLEAS AND TICKS

Your home environment determines to a great extent your dog's health and well-being. Keeping that environment free of fleas and ticks will eliminate a great deal of discomfort for your dog and some serious diseases for the humans as well as the dogs in your house.

Plan to make tick and flea detection part of your daily routine during the seasons when these pests are active in your part of the country.

Heavy infestations of fleas

Fleas and ticks can attach themselves to your dog when he is outside. Make sure to check your dog regularly for these parasites.

adulthood and jump onto a passing dog. The cycle resumes and usually takes between 21 to 28 days. Ask your veterinarian about environmental products that will kill both the adult flea and the larvae, and about products that are effective and safe to use on your dog.

Tick-borne disease has become a major health problem. Several varieties of ticks cause dangerous illnesses in animals and humans.

The American dog tick (*Dermacentor variablis*), also called the wood tick, can be found in woods and grassy areas across the US, but is most common on the East Coast. It carries Rocky Mountain Spotted Fever, erlichiosis and babesiosis, which is also known as pyroplasmosis. There is not yet a vaccine for these diseases. This tick also can cause tick paralysis, which usually occurs when a number of ticks have attached themselves to a dog that is outdoors most of the time. A

Feed your pup small amounts of food formulated for puppies several times a day.

toxin in the female tick causes the dog to stagger and collapse within a few days of being bitten. It's important to note that prompt removal of the ticks can reverse this paralysis within hours.

The deer tick (*Ixodes dammini*) carries babesiosis and Lyme disease. Two West Coast ticks, the western black-legged tick (*Ixodies pacificus*) and *Ixodies*

can cause anemia, which can lead to death in small dogs and puppies. If your dog is allergic to fleas, only one bite can cause "hot spots" that itch and burn.

If you check and treat the flea population daily, you may avoid a major infestation later on. Part your dog's coat and look for "flea dirt," the fleas' black fecal matter that clings to the dog's skin. As you run the metal flea comb through your dog's coat, watch for shiny black or dark brown shapes that quickly head for cover in deeper fur. They like the thick cover along your dog's back and around the tail.

As you catch fleas in the comb, drop them into a dish of ammonia or alcohol mixed with dish detergent. Treat your dog with flea powder or spray.

As adult fleas feast on your dog, they drop their eggs into the surrounding environment. They go through four larval stages before they reach

Nylabone® makes many different types of chew toys, including the Nylafloss™, that will provide your dog with hours of entertainment.

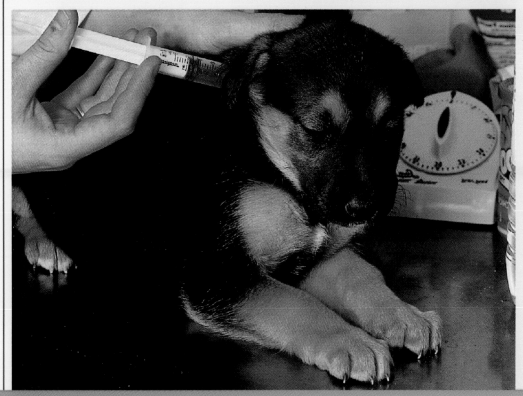

Get your adopted dog off to a good start. Bring him to a veterinarian within 48 hours after adoption.

summer, when mature ticks attach themselves; and in autumn, until a killing frost discourages activity. During these times, a tick preventive collar, dip or spray can discourage the potentially deadly arachnids. Also, sprays can control tick populations in outdoor areas. Consult your veterinarian on any course of action.

You are also susceptible to tick-borne disease, which can be life-threatening. If your dog has picked up ticks, you could, too. Take sensible

subscapularis, also carry Lyme. Symptoms are fever, loss of appetite, lethargy, lymph node enlargement, joint pain and lameness. A canine vaccine for Lyme, estimated to be 80 percent effective, is available in states where the disease is widespread.

The prolific brown dog tick (*Rhipicephalus sanguineus*), which can transmit babesiosis and erlichiosis, is a common kennel resident. It lays 2,000 to 4,000 eggs at a time. This is not a tick you want in your house. Check your dog carefully for this pest, especially if he has been in contact with dogs that stay in kennels.

Make sure to examine all pets before allowing them indoors. Backcomb your dog's hair to look for these pests.

Examine him for tiny feeding deer ticks, especially around the eyes, chin, anus and genitalia. Look in the ears and all around the body for dog ticks. If you find a tick, remove it with tweezers, exerting a slow, steady pull. Try not to leave mouth parts under the dog's skin. Put the tick on a piece of clear tape and show it to the vet for identification.

If your dog has been bitten, check his mouth daily. Pale gums indicate anemia, which could be caused by babesiosis or ehrlichiosis, both of which destroy blood cells. Without delay, take him to the veterinarian for testing and possible treatment.

Ticks are most active in the spring when the nymphs, some no bigger than poppy seeds, are feeding; during the

Tick-borne disease has become a major health problem in certain areas of the USA. Discuss your options with your vet.

Bringing a dog into the family can teach children the responsibility of owning a pet.

precautions: Wear light colors outdoors so ticks are easy to spot, tuck your pants into your socks, wear a hat in the woods, spray your shoes and socks with tick repellant and check yourself carefully before entering the house. Discourage ticks from taking up residence on your property by keeping grass mowed and preventing thatch from forming.

THE VETERINARIAN

Give your new dog a good start. Whether you adopt him from a shelter, not-for-profit agency, breeder or all-breed rescue network, take him to the veterinarian within 48 hours after adoption. Take a stool sample so the vet can check for internal parasites such as hookworms and roundworms. He or she may take some blood for a heartworm test. The animal

doctor will examine the dog thoroughly and make sure all inoculations are up to date. He will advise you when to come in for regular shots, and answer any questions you have about caring for your new dog. Many vets offer free examinations to adopted shelter dogs on their first visit.

To keep your dog healthy, schedule regular visits to your veterinarian.

To ensure your adopted dog's good health, schedule regular visits with your veterinarian.

The sky is the limit for an All-American dog. This Lab-Golden mix is a trusted seeing eye dog companion.

BASIC TRAINING FOR YOUR DOG

HOUSETRAINING

The best way to house train your puppy or adopted dog is to use the crate. Dogs do not like to relieve themselves where they eat and sleep, so your job is already half done if you use the crate to help teach appropriate behavior. Buy a crate that's large enough for your dog to stand and move around. There are wire crates and fiberglass crates, and each has its advantages. Choose whichever you like best. To accustom your dog to the crate, make it comfortable. Put an old towel or blanket in it as well as a favorite toy, and put him in it for just a few minutes at a time at first, increasing his stays gradually.

Puppies and adopted dogs both should be housetrained from square one. You've already introduced your dog or puppy to his crate the first day he is home. You've also taken him outside every two hours to relieve himself. Puppies need to go out more often than older dogs, but if your dog has been in a shelter, he's probably picked up undesirable habits, so you might as well start from scratch and housetrain him as you would a puppy.

After a few days, leave your dog in the crate for longer intervals. Feed and give him water in the crate. Whenever you let him out of the crate, take him directly outdoors. If he's in the yard, watch him until he takes care of his business. Notice the location he likes to use, and take him to it every time. Use a cue, such as "Poopies!" When he finishes, praise him: "Good Cody! What a good boy Cody is!" Then take him inside.

Training your dog should be a fun experience for you and your dog. Lady, a Pomeranian mix, is obeying the stay command.

If your dog is friendly and well-mannered like Chub Hummelsheim, you may want to take him through the Canine Good Citizen test.

When you're out for a walk and he relieves himself, praise him and head for home. He'll soon get the idea if you are consistent. Dogs respond to a routine. Let him know he can depend on you to help him do what is right.

When he is in the house, watch him. If you catch him in the act, or seconds after he has eliminated, scoop up the stool in a paper towel or wipe up the urine. Show it to him, or as you're picking it up, make a growling sound and say, "Bad poopies in house! Baaad poopies!" or something to that effect. If you don't keep an eye on him and the feces are cold by the time you discover them, you can try this, but it won't have the same effect. Don't rub his nose in it and don't physically punish him. If he sees how upset you are at what he's done, he'll get the idea. He may recognize his own stool by scent, but he won't be able to connect its existence with his behavior

of an hour ago.

Never use his name in this context. He is not a bad dog. Associate the punitive tone with what you found on the floor, not with your dog's name.

Paper training is useful if your dog will be alone for more than a few hours. Again, the crate is a valuable aid in teaching correct behavior. Spread newspaper over the floor in the room where he will stay while you

are out. For male dogs, who like to have something to urinate against, put a cardboard box in the middle of the newspaper.

After your dog's nap or after a meal in the crate, take him out and put him on the paper. When he does what he's supposed to, praise him to the skies. Each day, remove some of the newspaper from around the edges until there is one spot in the room where he will go on the newspapers each day.

Accidents will happen, and even the best-trained dog will have intestinal upsets or reasons, such as illness or stress, for frequent urination. Don't be punitive. Quietly and calmly remind him of the appropriate behavior, and if he isn't feeling well, consult with your veterinarian, and give him an extra cuddle.

CANINE GOOD CITIZEN

Training your dog is going to be one of the most rewarding experiences you've ever had. If you're responsible and diligent about going to classes and practicing every

Fully retractable leads are available in different strengths (and lengths) to allow owners to match the lead to the size and weight of their dogs. Photo courtesy of Flexi USA, Inc.

leash while owner goes out of sight.

Once you've learned the exercises leading to the CGC test, you might decide to go on to more demanding obedience exercises. It's fun and challenging to work your dog yourself, doing whatever you both enjoy. Like Arthur and Rick, you and your shelter dog could bring home ribbons from next year's agility meets.

COME

This is the most important command you'll ever teach your dog. It's essential to his safety. It will keep him from running off and becoming lost. It will keep him from running in front of a car. And, most important from his viewpoint, it will call him to dinner.

Once your dog masters the Sit command, as Sarge demonstrates, he is ready to move on to the Stay command.

day at home, you'll have not only a beautifully behaved dog, but also a devoted companion who knows what you expect of him and is eager to please you. You can even look forward to having a four-legged teammate for agility matches and obedience competitions.

But first things first. You want your dog to walk beside you when you take him out. He should learn to behave when he's at home, in public places and in the company of adults, children and other dogs.

If there are obedience classes near you, sign up. You and your dog will both learn, and he'll socialize with other dogs.

The AKC recognizes well-mannered dogs with its Canine Good Citizen

certification. Your trainer can help you prepare for the CGC test, or you can order the CGC pamphlet from the American Kennel Club and try a do-it-yourself approach. The test is often administered at dog shows. Both purebred and all-American dogs are eligible. The AKC can tell you about an organization in your area that gives the test.

The 10-part test includes exercises on:

Accepting a friendly stranger.

Sitting politely for petting.

Appearance and grooming.

Walking on lead.

Walking in a crowd.

Sit-stay and down-stay.

Interaction.

Reaction to another dog.

Reaction to distractions.

Allowing someone to hold

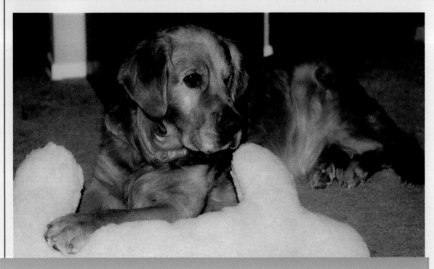

Buddy, a Golden Retriever adopted through Golden Rescue of St. Louis, loves his fleece bone.

Start teaching the come command on your adopted dog's first day home. As soon as he has his name, say it and follow it with "Come!" If he ignores you, tie a 20-foot rope to his collar. Go outdoors, and let him run around at the end of the rope. Then say "Come!" and reel him in. When he's right in front of you, praise him and give him a treat. Do this over and over again, every single day. Even after he comes on command almost every time, keep doing this until it's automatic.

Some dogs forget everything they've learned when they catch the scent of a deer or rabbit. You can yell "Come!" until you're blue in the face and they'll do nothing but "Go." Check your fence regularly to make sure it's secure, always keep your dog on a leash when you're out walking and instruct everyone who goes in and out of the house to look both ways before opening a door and

A new training system can get your dog's attention with a high-pitched whistle instead of the snap or pull of a chain collar. Photo courtesy of Wonder Whistle. For the location of the pet dealer nearest you, phone 800-633-3370.

Awaiting adoption at the Quincy Humane Society. "I've got a nice soft bed here, but I'd rather go home with you."

then to close it firmly behind them.

HEEL

After your dog has grown accustomed to the collar and lead, it's time to teach him to stay close to your left side, under your control at all times. This is especially important for his safety in areas where there is high pedestrian and vehicular

The Sit command is essential to your dog's basic training.

traffic. It is also the first thing you'll have to know when working toward CGC or obedience points. The command is "Heel," said in a firm voice just before stepping out. It's never necessary to raise your voice when training your dog.

Either the leather or chain collar can be used in teaching your dog to heel. However, never use a chain collar on a puppy less than six months old. Start with your dog by your left side, less than a foot away, facing the same direction. Hold the leash in your right hand, with the loop over your wrist. Hold it about halfway down with your left hand so that you can feel the dog's movements through the leash and adjust it accordingly. Your dog should walk along with you, close to your side. If he lags behind, give the collar a slight, quick snap — be extra careful not to snap too strongly with small dogs — and make cheerful sounds to encourage him to catch up with you. Stop snapping the instant the leash

becomes loose. Always work your dog on a loose leash. But be ready to tighten it if he starts to pull. Never drag your dog. You're teaching heel, not pull.

Sometimes tidbits help in training a puppy or young rambunctious dog. A good method that's easy on your back is to wedge a bit of cocktail sausage or liver between the fingers of a back scratcher. Hold the back scratcher down by your left leg just ahead of where you want your pup to be, and watch him follow along. After a good heel, reward him with praise and a treat.

While training your dog to heel, keep looking down at him. When he looks up at you, praise him. "Goooood Blitzen. Goooood heel!"

SIT

The sit command is essential to keep dogs politely in place while you talk with a friend, to prevent them from jumping on people and to stop them when they're about to get into trouble. Watch your new

dog and see how often he sits. He likes that position. When you tell him, "Sit," you're helping him do something he likes to do anyway. Cut up liver bits into tiny pieces to use as bait. Take a piece in your right hand and touch his nose with it. Then raise it slightly above his nose, so he'll have to raise his head. As he does this, his natural inclination is to sit. Simple, isn't it?

If you need to give him a little encouragement, run your hand gently along his back, pushing ever so slightly on his rump. Never press down heavily on his back. This adds an unpleasant dimension to what should be a positive learning experience. Don't

The Heel command teaches your dog to walk at your side and under control at all times.

forget to praise. "Goood Kipper! Oooh, what a good dog Kipper is. Good sit!"

Repeat the sit exercise several times every day, and soon it will be automatic behavior.

After your dog has learned to sit on command, teach him to stay in a sitting position and a standing position. Teach him the down command. A good book on training and an experienced dog trainer can help you and your dog learn commands that will enable you to take him almost everywhere with you and contribute to his enjoyment and safety. His actions might encourage others to become more responsible dog owners.

PROBLEM BEHAVIOR

"Not enough time" is the most frequent reason given by dog owners for giving up their dogs and breaking the human-canine bond. If an owner doesn't start out by

The Down command can be given to prevent all kinds of unwanted behaviors.

giving his dog the attention and training the animal deserves, he shouldn't be surprised when the untrained dog's behavior becomes first an annoyance and then an excuse for a one-way trip to the shelter. Your adopted dog may be a big bundle of love, but he will probably arrive with a problem or two in that bundle. Never fear. With love, patience and consistency— and time—you can retrain your new dog.

Correct undesirable behavior right away. Substitute correct behavior in a way your dog understands. For example, an effective way to stop your dog from jumping on a visitor is to give him a quick squirt

from a water pistol. This quickly takes his attention away from the person he's about to jump on. Where did that come from? He looks around to see. You haven't touched him, and he can't figure it out. His hesitation gives you a chance to get between him and the visitor. Command him to sit. Then the visitor can get down to his level and greet him without fuss. If he hasn't learned the sit command yet, give him a squeaky toy to distract him. What a good dog!

Never knee him or step on his feet to get him to stop jumping. This will only make him fear you, and you might injure him.

Agility training is a great way to channel your dog's energy into a fun exercise.

This all-American dog awaits his new owner at the shelter. Could it be you?

In the course of his day, your puppy will want to eat, play, exercise and nap often.

CHEWING

Dogs chew. It's a fact of life. Puppies chew when they're teething. They also chew because they're intelligent, curious critters, and they put objects in their mouths to get information about them. Adult dogs chew out of curiosity, but also because chewing is a deep-rooted instinct. They chew for other reasons, too: boredom, anger, frustration, pure devilment.

There are some effective ways for you to train your dog away from problem shredding to appropriate chewing activities. Give him plenty of exercise as a positive outlet for his energy, so he'll be more likely to nap than to chew when he's out of your sight. After an hour of chasing Gumabone® Frisbees®, he'll happily collapse, his tongue lolling out. Toss him a tooth-tempting frozen carrot to cool him off.

Vigorous exercise will also discourage your dog from other inappropriate behavior such as digging, excessive barking, pacing and whining. Give him good chew toys to keep him out of trouble. Some toys that will give your dog's teeth and jaws a good workout are super-tough Hercules®, Nylarings® and tasty liver-flavored Nylabones®. Praise your dog for good chewing behavior.

AGGRESSION

Neutering is the best remedy for male aggression, which usually takes the form of fights over territory, social pecking order or a female in heat. Spaying is the best solution for bitches who will fight both females and males over possessions and social dominance within the pack. Of course, if these procedures haven't been performed before adoption, spaying and neutering are the only responsible actions for a non-breeder to take when he or she adopts a dog. But even neutered dogs display aggression, usually because they haven't been properly socialized or because they have been treated harshly by a former owner.

Aggression begets aggression. If you tie your

Above: A well-adjusted, temperamentally sound and spayed or neutered dog will not be prone to aggression. *Below:* Thanks to his new owner this all-American gets to relax on the chaise lounge.

Agility training is a great way to get exercise for both dog and owner.

dog outside or beat him, he'll respond by becoming more aggressive. You can defuse a potentially explosive situation between dogs by acting calm and unconcerned. Try to prevent fights by allowing dogs to greet each other naturally, on loose leashes. If snarling or lunging starts, gather up your dog's leash and let him know, in gentle but firm tones, that you are now leaving.

Never try to separate fighting dogs. You may be bitten in the process, or they may even turn on you. If a hose is nearby, spray them, if you can do so without getting close to them. If your dog is injured, take him to the veterinarian immediately. Your vet's regular and emergency phone numbers should be taped to your phones.

If your adopted dog

shows aggression toward people, consult your veterinarian or a trainer specializing in dog behavior.

Make sure to properly socialize your dog and train him in obedience. Shelters and rescue organizations carefully evaluate dogs for aggressive tendencies, so it is unlikely that you will have this problem. However, if your adopted dog threatens you or a member of your family, and does not respond to gentle correction and a secure, loving home environment, don't feel guilty about giving him up. You can't afford to endanger your family. And there are other deserving dogs waiting for adoption. You've prepared yourself, your family and your home. You're committed to devoting the time and energy it will take to help your dog become a happy, healthy member of your household. You deserve the dog that's best for you. And that dog deserves a loving, responsible best friend like you.

Toad, an Airedale-Shepherd mix, is very tolerant of these curious youngsters.

All dogs deserve loving homes and owners.

SUGGESTED READING

TS-205
Successful Dog Training
160 pages, 130 full-color
photos.

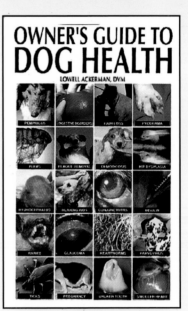

TS-214
Owner's Guide to Dog Health
432 pages, over 300 full-color
photos.

TS-175
Andrew DePrisco &
James B. Johnson
896 pages, over 1300
full-color photographs.

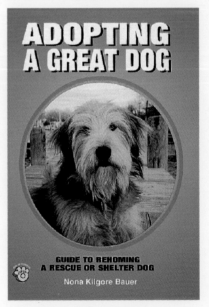

TS-293
Nona Kilgore Bauer
183 pages, full-color
photos throughout.